A Nest Full of Eggs

by Priscilla Belz Jenkins
illustrated by Lizzy Rockwell

HarperCollins*Publishers*

To my mother, with love —P. B. J.
For Ken —L. R.

Special thanks to Dr. Charles Walcott for his expert advice.

The illustrations for this book were done in pencil and watercolor on T.H. Saunders watercolor paper.

The *Let's-Read-and-Find-Out Science* book series was originated by Dr. Franklyn M. Branley, Astronomer Emeritus and former Chairman of the American Museum–Hayden Planetarium, and was formerly co-edited by him and Dr. Roma Gans, Professor Emeritus of Childhood Education, Teachers College, Columbia University. Text and illustrations for each of the books in the series are checked for accuracy by an expert in the relevant field. For a complete catalog of Let's-Read-and-Find-Out Science books, write to HarperCollins Children's Books, 10 East 53rd Street, New York, NY 10022.

Let's Read-and-Find-Out Science is a registered trademark of HarperCollins Publishers.

3/25/97   B&T   14.89/12.54

Library of Congress Cataloging-in-Publication Data
Jenkins, Priscilla Belz.
  A nest full of eggs / by Priscilla Belz Jenkins ; illustrated by Lizzy Rockwell.
    p.   cm. — (Let's-read-and-find-out science. Stage 1)
  ISBN 0-06-023441-5. — ISBN 0-06-023442-3 (lib. bdg.)
  ISBN 0-06-445127-5 (pbk.)
  1. Robins—Juvenile literature.   2. Parental behavior in animals—Juvenile literature.   3. Eggs—Juvenile
literature. [1. Robins. 2. Eggs. 3. Parental behavior in animals.] I. Rockwell, Lizzy, ill. II. Title. III. Series.
QL696.P288J46 1995   93-43804
598.8'42—dc20   CIP
                                                                    AC

A Nest Full of
Eggs

Listen. "Cheer-up, cheer-up, cheer-up." That is the song of a robin. It must be spring!

Up in a tree outside my window, a pair of American robins is very busy. They are gathering dry weeds and twigs. They work carefully but quickly. It is almost time.

The female weaves the weeds
and twigs together with bits of
mud that dry like glue.

She adds more mud, pressing it
with her breast into a cup shape.

Then she lines the bottom of
the cup with a bed of soft grasses.

There. The nest is strong, safe, and snug.

Now it is ready.

Over the next few days, the female robin lays four beautiful blue eggs in the nest. She is sitting on the nest now, keeping the eggs warm. Her mate is close by. He sings loudly, warning other robins to stay away.

9

Inside each egg is a tiny new life. It is growing very fast. The yellow yolk is its liquid food. The clear albumen, which we call the "white" of an egg, is its watery cushion. Day after day, the mother robin sits on the eggs, patiently waiting.

IT MUST BE NICE AND WARM IN THERE.

THAT WHITE SPOT IN THE MIDDLE IS THE BEGINNING OF LIFE.

IN AN EGG

air sac

yolk

shell

albumen

3 DAYS

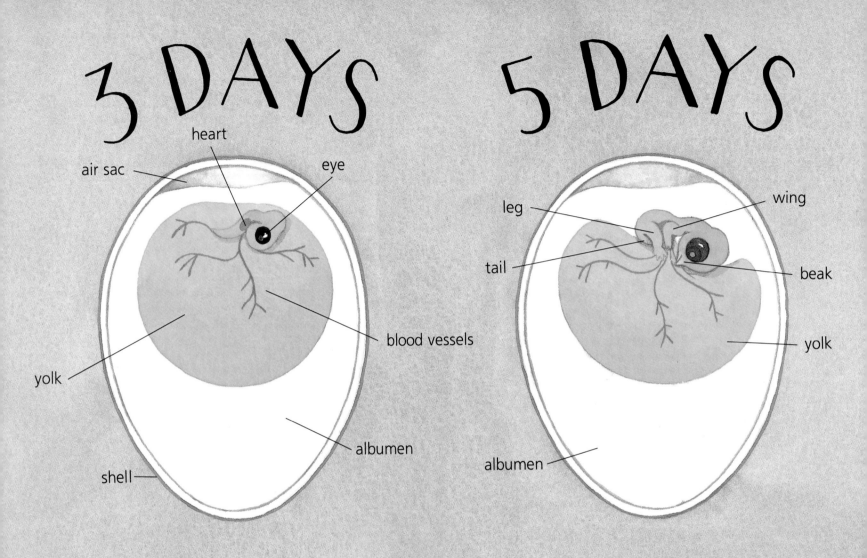

air sac

heart

eye

yolk

blood vessels

albumen

shell

5 DAYS

leg

wing

tail

beak

yolk

albumen

After three days, the life begins to look like a head, a backbone, a heart, and eyes. Already the heart is beating.

After five days, a beak, two wings, two legs, and a tail are taking shape. It is beginning to look like a baby bird in there.

8 DAYS

12 DAYS

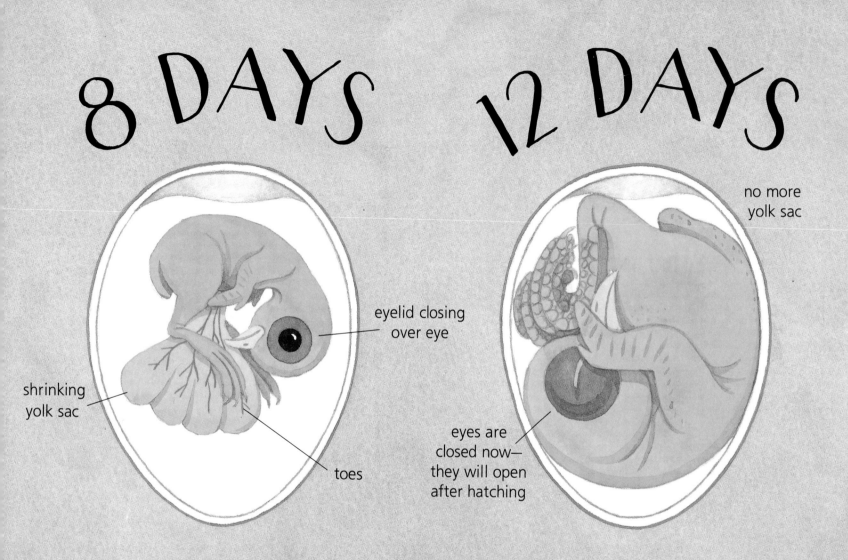

shrinking
yolk sac

eyelid closing
over eye

toes

no more
yolk sac

eyes are
closed now—
they will open
after hatching

After about eight days,
the robin is completely formed,
right down to its toes.

By the twelfth day, the robin
has grown so big, it is squeezed
inside the egg. It has used up all
the food and space.

Listen. "Peep. Peep. Peep-peep." A tiny beak is breaking through an eggshell. The eggs are hatching!

Crack! Out rolls a baby robin. Soon there are four wobbly little robins in the nest. Their parents feed them worms, berries, seeds, and insects. But the hungry nestlings are always peeping and squawking for more food.

15

In a few days, the baby robins open their eyes. Soft, warm down feathers begin to appear on their bodies.

Then bigger feathers grow and cover the down. They keep the robins dry and give them color and shape.

About fourteen days after hatching, the robins have grown their wing and tail feathers. These are their "flight" feathers—the feathers that they will use to fly.

Feathers are light but very strong. They are what makes birds so different from all other creatures on earth. Only birds have feathers. Feathers come in many sizes, shapes, and colors.

WE FOUND THESE IN THE YARD.

LET'S LOOK THIS ONE UP.

FEATHERS OF THE BIRDS

ORIOLE

FLAMINGO

BIRD OF PARADISE

GUINEA FOWL

FINCH

CEDAR WAXWING

CURLEW

PARROT

PEACOCK

BLUE JAY

JUNCO

HUMMINGBIRD

SPOTTED WOODPECKER

MANDARIN DUCK

PARAKEET

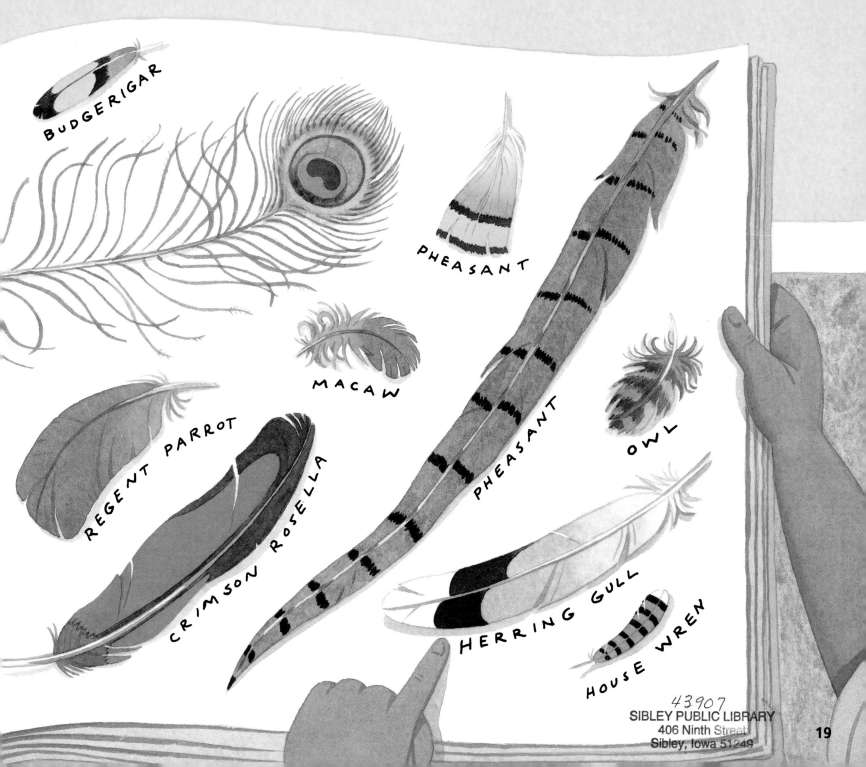

BUDGERIGAR

PHEASANT

MACAW

REGENT PARROT

CRIMSON ROSELLA

PHEASANT

OWL

HERRING GULL

HOUSE WREN

OUCH!

ROBIN

Robins, like all birds, take good care of their feathers. They comb them and straighten them with their beaks.

SPARROW TAKING A DUST BATH

IF WE WERE BIRDS THIS WOULD BE OUR BATH.

HOUSE FINCH

COWBIRD

And they clean them by taking baths in water or dust.

GOLDFINCH

21

GETTING A BIT CROWDED...

TAKING A STRETCH...

Now the young robins are ready to leave their nest. But they are not good fliers yet. They are still learning. For the next few weeks their parents stay close to them and bring them food.

AND AWAY WE GO!

Soon the robins are ready to fly and hunt on their own. Now they can take care of themselves. Next spring they will find mates and have nests of their own.

Birds live all over the world. There are about 9,000 different kinds. Each kind of bird makes a nest in its own special way. Birds usually hide their nests where they blend with nature's colors.

A bird's nest can be:

WHIP-POOR-WILL

a gathering of leaves on the forest floor

NORTHERN FLICKER

a hole in a tree

NORTHERN ORIOLE

a woven pouch

PEREGRINE FALCON

a scrape on a rocky cliff top

BALD EAGLE

a gigantic heap of branches

RED NECKED GREBE

a floating platform

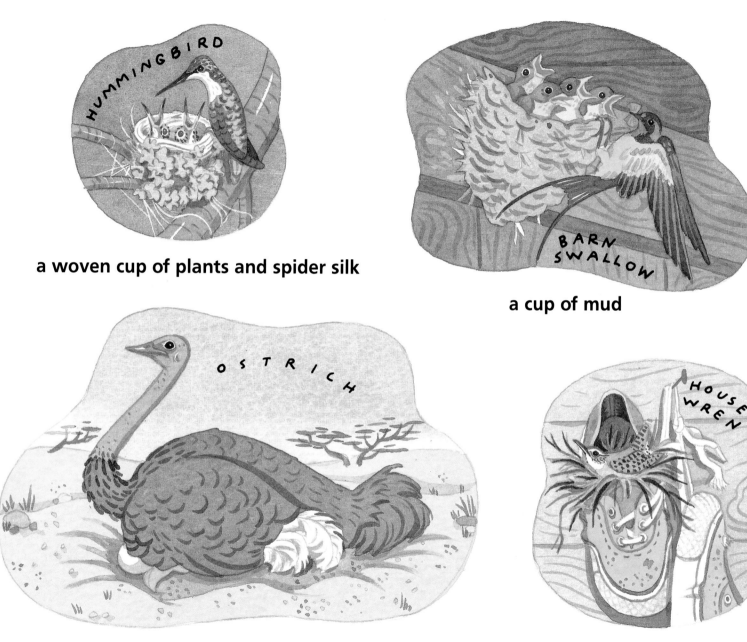

HUMMINGBIRD

a woven cup of plants and spider silk

BARN SWALLOW

a cup of mud

OSTRICH

a scooped-out hollow in the sand

HOUSE WREN

or even an old shoe!

NEWSPAPER

STRING

GRASS CLIPPINGS

28

You can help robins build their nests. In the spring, leave some grass clippings and bits of yarn and string in your yard. Look for robins picking them up. Watch where they go. You may be able to find their nest. Help the robins feel safe by not going too close to the nest or touching it. See if you can tell if the eggs have hatched.

YARN

HAIR

DRIED WEEDS

SHREDDED NEWSPAPER

CELLOPHANE

LOON

CROW

MURRE

EMU

ROBIN

WREN

HAWK

GULL

As summer ends in late
September and the days grow
shorter, the robins fly south, or
migrate. They know it is time to
leave. Winter is coming.

BIRDS

But the robins always return. Listen.
"Cheer-up, cheer-up, cheer-up."
Spring is here again.